W9-BNV-397

MICROSOFT

ABDO
Publishing Company

TECHNOLOGY
PIONEERS

MICROSOFT

THE COMPANY AND ITS FOUNDERS

by Ashley Rae Harris

Content Consultant
Jeffrey R. Yost
Associate Director, Charles Babbage Institute,
University of Minnesota

CREDITS

Published by ABDO Publishing Company, PO Box 398166,
Minneapolis, MN 55439. Copyright © 2013 by Abdo Consulting
Group, Inc. International copyrights reserved in all countries.
No part of this book may be reproduced in any form without
written permission from the publisher. The Essential Library™ is a
trademark and logo of ABDO Publishing Company.

Printed in the United States of America,
North Mankato, Minnesota
052012
092012

 THIS BOOK CONTAINS AT LEAST 10% RECYCLED MATERIALS.

Editor: Sue Vander Hook
Series Designer: Emily Love

Library of Congress Cataloging-in-Publication Data
Harris, Ashley Rae.
  Microsoft : the company and its founders / Ashley Rae Harris.
    p. cm. -- (Technology pioneers)
  ISBN 978-1-61783-333-5
  1. Microsoft Corporation--History--Juvenile literature. 2. Gates,
Bill, 1955---Juvenile literature. 3. Allen, Paul, 1953---Juvenile
literature. 4. Computer software industry--United States--Juvenile
literature I. Title.
  HD9696.63.U64M53615 2013
  338.7'610040973--dc23
                                      2012010835

TABLE OF CONTENTS

Microsoft's first 11 employees, including Bill Gates, *lower left*, and Paul Allen, *lower right*, are on display at the Microsoft Visitor Center.

SOFTWARE START-UP TO SUPERSTAR

Aboard an airplane in September 1980, Bill Gates and coworkers Steve Ballmer and Bob O'Rear were nervous wrecks. They were on their way to one of the largest computer companies in the world—IBM. None of them had slept for several days. They had been too busy preparing for the most important meeting of their young careers. The overnight flight from Seattle, Washington, to Miami, Florida, provided little time for rest as they anxiously tweaked and rehearsed their presentation. They would soon deliver it in a conference room filled with seasoned business executives in expensive suits. If the meeting went well, it could transform their small software company, Microsoft. It could also change their lives forever.

The meeting with IBM was the opportunity Gates and his partner, Paul Allen, had been waiting for. The two of them had started Microsoft five years before, in the spring of 1975, when Gates was only 20 years old and Allen was 22. Microsoft's main business was developing software for microcomputers. In a short amount of time, their little company had grown from just the two of them to approximately 40 employees.

Microsoft was making a decent profit, at least enough to afford new suits for Gates, Ballmer, and O'Rear for their meeting in Florida. The young Microsoft team normally worked in jeans, T-shirts, and sneakers. They were becoming well known, especially among their fellow computer fanatics.

IBM

Founded in 1911 as the Computing Tabulating Recording Co., the company adopted the name International Business Machines (IBM) in 1924. It originally made equipment that helped companies record and process data such as employee records. In the 1950s, IBM expanded its computer technology to collect and process various data for big government organizations. IBM equipment also tracked space orbits for NASA. Until the 1980s, IBM machines were massive mainframes and somewhat large minicomputers. In 1981, the company released the IBM PC with the Microsoft operating system MS-DOS. It became the first widely sold personal computer for the home. Today, IBM ranks as the eighteenth-largest company in the United States and the thirty-first in the world, with $100 billion in sales and more than 400,000 employees. The company, sometimes called Big Blue, manufactures computer hardware and software and offers technical support and consulting services in areas from mainframes to artificial intelligence. IBM also manufactures parts for most major gaming systems, such as Xbox 360, Wii, and Sony PlayStation. Microsoft and IBM continue to compete for the market share in computer software and related business areas.

But no one could have predicted the Microsoft explosion that lay ahead.

FIRST MEETING IN SEATTLE

The trip to Florida was not the first meeting between Microsoft and IBM. Several months earlier, IBM executives had shown up at Microsoft's office in Seattle to meet Gates. At first, they were not impressed. Gates was dressed in a rumpled T-shirt and jeans and looked more like a teenager than a young man in his twenties. The IBM representatives were dumbfounded that this small, messy-haired kid was chief executive officer (CEO) of the company. They wondered if their trip had been a waste of time and money. But their worries soon passed when Gates began talking. It was clear he was a computer whiz and very knowledgeable about computer software. They were convinced Gates would be able to help them with a very important project.

IBM was known for building massive mainframe computers used mostly in government offices and big corporations. Now IBM had created a small computer that it planned to market to individuals for personal use. However, the company needed software to operate this new personal computer (PC). Word was out that Microsoft, a new up-and-coming company, could provide what IBM needed.

The job sounded fairly straightforward at first. But after talking to Gates, the IBM people realized there was more work to be done than they originally imagined. IBM had a very specific idea for

MAINFRAMES

Mainframe computers, called Giant Brains in their early years, were first built in the 1950s. By the 1960s, these extremely large computers, with their massive memory and data storage, had become a vital tool for many government institutions and major corporations. During the 1970s and 1980s, most mainframes were replaced with minicomputers and PCs. However, with the emergence of the Internet, mainframes became popular again, used by online businesses to store and process large amounts of data.

IBM introduced its first personal computer, the 5150, in August 1981.

the type of PC it would sell, the chip that would power it, and the speed at which it would run. It was immediately clear to Gates that the PC required a new operating system, and he told them so.

OPPORTUNITY OF A LIFETIME

Microsoft was good at creating software, but building operating systems was not its specialty at that time. If Microsoft was going to get this job and meet IBM's timetable, Gates was going to have to find someone who had an operating system that would work for the PC. It was a huge opportunity for Microsoft and something Gates was not about to pass up.

Gates called an old business contact, Gary Kildall, to see if he was interested in teaming up.

The two men had known each other for a number of years and had helped each other's businesses grow. Recently they had not been seeing eye-to-eye, but Gates needed what Kildall had. Digital Research, Kildall's company, had an operating system he believed could work with Microsoft software and get IBM's PC up and running quickly. Gates convinced Kildall to take advantage of this huge opportunity.

IBM executives met with Digital Research, but the experience left a sour taste in their mouths. While Gates had impressed IBM with his smarts and charm, the people at Digital Research had seemed uncooperative and possibly incapable of providing an operating system. When IBM decided they could not work with Digital Research, it seemed as if the remarkable opportunity was about to vanish right before Gates's eyes.

QUICK AND DIRTY OPERATING SYSTEM

Just down the street from Microsoft's Seattle office, a small company called Seattle Computer

DIGITAL RESEARCH

Digital Research, a software and operating systems company founded in 1976 by Gary Kildall and his wife, Dorothy McEwen, competed with Microsoft throughout the 1980s. The company was sold in 1991 to Novell, a software company that wanted rights to the company's operating system.

Products was developing a new operating system called QDOS, which stood for Quick and Dirty Operating System. It was soon renamed 86-DOS. Gates was almost certain that with modifications, 86-DOS would run IBM's PC. Microsoft paid the company for full rights to use the operating system. Microsoft might be able to make the IBM deal work after all.

For the next few months, Microsoft employees worked around the clock to modify 86-DOS. They lived on Coca-Cola and pizza and slept in the office. They had to convince IBM they had a workable operating system. Finally, they were ready to present their work to IBM.

While Allen stayed in Seattle to keep Microsoft going, Gates, Ballmer, and O'Rear boarded an airplane for Miami where they met for the second time with IBM. There, Gates presented MS-DOS, the name Microsoft gave its new operating system that would run IBM's PC. Eventually MS-DOS and subsequent Microsoft operating systems would run 90 percent of the world's computers and make Gates the richest man in the world. The deal with IBM was the spark that would ignite Microsoft and turn it into one of the most powerful multinational companies in the world. +

Gates grew his small computer company into an industry giant.

Gates at age 29 in 1984

BORN TO SUCCEED

Most people give credit to Gates for the incredible success of Microsoft. He started the company at the age of 20, but the foundation for his success began many years before. As a young child, Gates had an extraordinary drive to be the best at everything he set out to do. His family encouraged his ambitions and had the resources to support them.

Gates was born William Henry Gates III on October 28, 1955, in Seattle, Washington. His parents were Mary Maxwell Gates and William Henry Gates II. He was the middle child, sandwiched between two sisters, Libby and Kristi.

The Gates family was well established in the community. Bill's father was an attorney, and his mother poured her energy into fund-raising for charitable causes. She often threw lavish parties where young Bill learned to socialize with Seattle's most powerful people. It was a skill that would come in handy later when he set out to convince the business world to accept his technology.

It was obvious to most who met young Bill that he was not an average child. He was an avid reader, devouring entire encyclopedias by the age of seven. Carl Edmark, Bill's closest childhood friend, once said, "Everything Bill did, he did to the max. . . . What he did always went well, well beyond everyone else."[1] Bill could also be rather quirky. He often rocked his body back and forth for long periods of time, especially if he was thinking deeply about something.

LAKESIDE SCHOOL

In 1967, when 11-year-old Bill was ready for seventh grade, his parents enrolled him in Lakeside School on the north side of Seattle. Lakeside was an exclusive private preparatory school for boys. Bill's parents knew he needed the academic challenges offered at Lakeside.

Lakeside made an interesting choice the year Bill enrolled. The school decided to teach the students how to use computers. Access to computers at school was unheard of at the time. The only computers that existed were mainframes that usually filled entire rooms or fairly large minicomputers. They cost hundreds of thousands or even millions of dollars and generally only

MARY GATES

Mary Gates, the mother of Bill Gates, had a profound influence on her son. Mary and her son were quite close, and he regularly sought her approval and advice. Once Microsoft was using e-mail, Gates had his mother's home computer connected to the company network so they could communicate throughout the day. Some have speculated that Mary's connections were key to Microsoft's breakthrough business deal with IBM. At that time, she was on the board for the charitable organization United Way alongside John Opel, IBM's CEO. She would later become United Way's first female president. When Microsoft later went public, the Gates family held a significant 114,000 shares in the company. Mary encouraged her son to share his extensive wealth and give back to society through philanthropy. Mary Gates died in 1994 at the age of 64.

the government or major corporations used them. Lakeside did not purchase a computer; instead, it paid for computer time on a large minicomputer owned by General Electric. Through bake sales and other fund-raising efforts, the Lakeside Mothers Club raised $3,000 to pay for the students' computer time.

Students first learned to type commands on a teleprinter located at the school. The teleprinter converted their typed messages to coded pulses, which were transmitted through telephone lines to a PDP-10 computer at General Electric in downtown Seattle. Students learned the basic principles of computing and how messages were transmitted. Bill and some of the other students were immediately fascinated by the computer and began using up the school's computer time very quickly. They spent so much time on the computer that their other schoolwork suffered.

Another student equally captivated by the teleprinter and the computer was Paul Allen,

THE TELEPRINTER

The teleprinter, developed in the early 1900s, is a typewriter-like keyboard that sends, receives, and prints coded data via wires, cables, radio waves, and other means of communication. With the advent of mainframe computers in the late 1950s, the teleprinter was used to transmit data to computers. The brand name, Teletype, became a common term for this machine, which is now nearly obsolete.

a soft-spoken teenager who loved the magazine *Popular Electronics*. Some students at the school described him as "more approachable and friendlier" than some of the other computer enthusiasts, including Bill.[2] Nonetheless, Bill and Paul met at school in 1968 and became good friends and fellow computer enthusiasts.

A DESIRE TO LEARN

Paul Allen, born on January 21, 1953, in Seattle, was two years older than Bill. His parents were Sam Allen, a librarian at the University of Washington, and Edna Faye Allen, a schoolteacher with a passion for reading. According to Paul's 2011 memoir, he started reading long before kindergarten. Throughout his childhood, he had a strong desire to learn about science, gasoline engines, electronics, weather, robots, and much more.

When Paul was nine years old, his parents took him to the 1962 Seattle World's Fair, where he plunged himself in the wonders of the science pavilion. He recalled, "I ran around like a kid on a sugar high—what to see next?"[3] His interest in science did not end with the fair; he visited science labs at universities and conducted his own chemistry

Bill Gates and Paul Allen used a Teletype machine
during their years at Lakeside School.

experiments in the basement of his home. Computers
also fascinated Paul. He had only read about them in
science fiction books. But when his parents enrolled
him at Lakeside School in the seventh grade, he got
his chance to try out a real computer.

WORKING AT C-CUBED

In 1968, a new company called Computer Center
Corporation offered a deal to Lakeside School. It was
similar to the deal with General Electric; the school
would pay Computer Center for students to use its
computers. While the arrangement was good for the

students, it was not so great for C-Cubed, the name Bill gave the company because of the three *C*s in the name. When students worked on the computers at the C-Cubed offices, they left them running too long and found programs they were not supposed to access. They also broke into the company's security system and discovered how to reduce the number of hours students actually used the computers. This reduced Lakeside's bill considerably. Bill and other students also learned how to make the computers crash, which Bill in particular found quite exciting.

C-Cubed was less than thrilled about its system crashing. However, the company's programmer Steve Russell and his colleagues realized it was important to find the flaws in the system and learn why the computers crashed. That way, they could quickly repair them. They decided to make a deal with Bill, Paul, Kent Evans, another Lakeside student named Rick Weiland, and Kildall, a computer science doctoral student. The five of them

SPACE WARS

Steve Russell, a computer programmer at C-Cubed, created the first computer video game with graphics in 1961. Russell spent many long, tedious hours creating *Space Wars* on the DEC PDP-1 computer at the Massachusetts Institute of Technology (MIT) in Cambridge. The graphics were very simple. Dots on the screen were stars, and players battled with rocket ships. Many later computer games were developed in the style of *Space Wars*. In the 1970s, a version of *Space Wars* was created for the video game company Atari.

could have all the precious computer time they wanted at no cost if they logged all the bugs in the system and reported them to C-Cubed. Essentially, the boys were being paid in computer time to make computers crash and find out why.

The group of five, who called themselves the Lakeside Programmers Group, became a tight-knit clique. Thirteen-year-old Bill and 15-year-old Paul spent day and night on the computers at C-Cubed. Whenever Russell checked on them, they bombarded him with questions. Sometimes he gave them old programming manuals, which they devoured from cover to cover.

Two years later, in 1970, C-Cubed went out of business, and Bill took a break from the Lakeside Programmers Group. Bill and Paul took jobs doing payroll programming for companies in exchange for free computer time. The two teenagers also created Logic Simulation Company, which generated computerized schedules for students at Lakeside.

Also that year, Bill and Paul came up with their first true moneymaking venture, Traf-O-Data. They discovered they could use a teleprinter and a computer to measure the flow of traffic. It was a big improvement over the old method of counting cars as they rode over rubber hoses. They created a binary code and a computer program that read the results. The data they gathered were sold in the form of flow charts to cities or other organizations to help with traffic control. Traf-O-Data earned them approximately $20,000 before they disbanded it.

When Paul graduated from Lakeside in 1971, he enrolled at Washington State University in Pullman, Washington. But he soon discovered he was not cut out for college. He dropped out to take a job as a programmer with TRW, a defense contracting company. When Bill was a senior at Lakeside, Paul recruited him to also join TRW. Lakeside allowed Bill to work at TRW for part of his senior year. Bill and Paul were again working together with computers. This time, however, they were not making computer systems crash; they were fixing them after they crashed.

In 1973, 17-year-old Bill graduated from Lakeside School and made plans to attend Harvard University in Cambridge, Massachusetts, in the fall. What he learned at Lakeside and the connections he made there would alter his life. His partnership with his friend Paul would not end at graduation. Together they would set out on a venture that would make them two of the most exceptional businessmen of all time. +

Allen and Gates no longer work together,
but they continue to be good friends.

CHAPTER 3

Microsoft cofounders Gates and Allen, *right*, combined college and business in the early 1970s.

FLEDGLING COMPANY

Before Gates left Lakeside School in 1973, he told his classmates he expected to become a millionaire by the age of 30. Since Gates was known for making bold statements about his future, the students shrugged and assumed he was probably right. After all, he already had a strong track record as a successful entrepreneur. But Gates's personal confidence was only part of the reason he would become so successful. The shared vision that Gates and his good friend Allen had for the technology of the future would be the key to their success.

Gates and Allen both believed that computers of the future would not just reside in corporate offices and government institutions. They believed computers would be in people's homes where they could become a regular part of daily life. Their vision would come true much sooner than they expected.

In the fall of 1973, Allen was still working as a programmer for TRW. Gates had just started his freshman year of college at Harvard University. He tried to get into the college lifestyle but found himself, as always, putting his energy into a few favorite activities. He took

UNIVERSITY POLICY

When Gates attended Harvard, he and Allen used university computers for their private projects that would one day make them a lot of money. The US Department of Defense owned and provided the computers for a specific research project. Later, the university came up with a new regulation that prevented students from using school property for their own commercial gains.

a graduate level math course but spent most of his time studying computer coding and playing poker. Over dinner in the cafeteria, he often talked about science fiction and engineering with fellow students who lived in the same residence hall.

Gates also developed odd sleeping habits at Harvard. He would stay up for 36 hours at a time and then sleep ten hours all at once. Sometimes he spoke computer coding language in his sleep. He never used sheets, a quirk that would stay with him the rest of his life. Gates was not the only one at Harvard with these strange sleeping habits. One of his close friends, Steve Ballmer, shared not only Gates's odd sleeping patterns but also his tendency to rock back and forth. Gates and Ballmer would become close friends and have a lifelong friendship and business relationship.

LET'S START A COMPANY

While Gates attended college, Allen looked for opportunities for the two of them to start a company. In the summer of 1974, they both worked in Boston, Massachusetts, for Honeywell, an engineering and technology company that made mainframe computers. Briefly, they considered starting a similar company but soon recognized that their strengths were in software. They continued to look for the right opportunity to use their skills.

In December, that opportunity came. In a convenience store, Allen happened to notice the cover of the new January 1975 issue of *Popular Electronics* magazine. The featured article was "World's First Microcomputer Kit to Rival Commercial Models."[1] The kit would provide all the parts so a person could make a personal home computer. It was called the Altair 8800. Right away, Gates and Allen knew this was

HISTORY OF SOFTWARE ENGINEERING

When computers were first being developed between 1955 and 1965, software commonly was rewritten for each new computer that was made. Scientists and businesspeople used computers that were programmed just for their needs; thus, their software was also distinct. During this time, the programming languages FORTRAN, COBOL, and ALGOL were created. Hardware companies such as IBM generally hired their own programmers to build system software for the computers. Programmers shared computers since no one had a private computer.

After 1965, the profession began to stabilize. IBM released the System/360 family of compatible computers, which allowed software programmers to move away from rewriting software applications for each new machine. The type of operating system on the computer determined how the software was programmed. In the 1960s and 1970s, a host of companies started making and selling software products and systems for minicomputers and mainframes. One of those companies was Microsoft, which also pioneered software for PCs and significantly changed the computer industry. It became the largest and most powerful company to sell just computer software.

MITS received approximately 1,000 orders for its
Altair 8800 computer kit in February 1975.

their opportunity. The computer was going to need
software in order to run.

Ed Roberts, one of the founders of Micro
Instrumentation and Telemetry Systems (MITS), had
developed the Altair 8800 kit. The main business
of MITS was making calculator kits, but the Altair
8800 was a very different device. The article said
each kit would cost $397, an incredibly cheap price
for a computer. The Altair 8800 would run on Intel
computer chips and have 256 bytes of memory,
with the possibility of 4,096 bytes if additional
memory boards were installed. MITS marketed it as
the "people's computer" that used BASIC software
language. However, the Altair 8800's BASIC

interpreter, which would decode the software, had not yet been developed.

Gates and Allen were ecstatic. BASIC software language was what they knew best. They were confident they could make a program that would work on the Altair. Gates called Roberts and told him he had a BASIC software program that would work on his computer. Actually, neither Gates nor Allen had written the program yet. Then they created a written proposal on their old Traf-O-Data letterhead. At first, Roberts blew off the call from Gates, assuming it was an empty boast like several others he had received. But Gates and Allen had already begun rapidly coding BASIC for the Altair 8800.

For the next several weeks, the two of them practically camped out in Harvard's Aiken Computer Lab. Gates worked on creating BASIC code that would use a tiny amount of memory. Previously he'd only coded for large mainframes, so this was a new and difficult challenge. Meanwhile, Allen worked on getting the PDP-10 in the lab to

BASIC SOFTWARE

BASIC stands for Beginner's All-Purpose Symbolic Instruction Code. It originated in the early days of computers when each computer needed customized software. It became a common programming language in the 1970s and was used as the basis for the software programs Microsoft designed.

act like the Intel chips so they could test their program. Next, they recruited Gates's Harvard classmate Monte Davidoff to help.

IT WORKS!

Eight weeks later, in March 1975, Gates and Allen were confident they had the right program, and they had tested it on the PDP-10. Allen made arrangements to fly to Albuquerque, New Mexico, and show it to Roberts at MITS. When he arrived at MITS, Allen was a little surprised. Although he had not expected an extremely huge office, he was shocked that MITS was just a tiny storefront in a strip mall between a laundromat and a massage parlor.

Allen quickly forgot about the less-than-fancy environment, however. He was getting ready to show Roberts the program he and Gates had developed. The teleprinter was connected to the Altair. As Allen loaded a long strip of paper tape punched with the BASIC code into the teleprinter, his nerves were on edge. Allen and Gates had never tested their program on the Altair or with that particular Intel chip. They had only simulated it on the PDP-10.

Suddenly, the lights on the Altair 8800 began flashing. Their program was working. All their hard work over the past months had paid off. Allen and Gates had successfully developed software that was now working on a very small computer.

Allen could not wait to tell Gates the good news. But before he left Albuquerque, he played a few rounds of the *Lunar Lander* game on the Altair. The game was an old favorite of the Lakeside Programmers Group. When Allen returned to Cambridge, the two young men, still under the age of 21, enjoyed ice cream and nonalcoholic cocktails to celebrate their success.

ALBUQUERQUE, HERE WE COME

Allen immediately moved to Albuquerque to work as software director for MITS. The company became profitable overnight once the *Popular Electronics* issue hit the newsstands. Some computer enthusiasts camped out in the MITS parking lot waiting for their kits to be ready to take home.

Gates and Allen quickly put together the legal documents to form their own software company.

They called it Micro-Soft. A year later, the hyphen was dropped, and the company became Microsoft. Allen owned 36 percent of the company, and Gates got 64 percent since he had done the majority of the work in creating the BASIC software program for the Altair. Gates had also taken a leadership role in Microsoft's negotiations with early clients.

Gates put together the contract with MITS. The agreement, which would last for several years, gave MITS the exclusive right to license the software Gates had created. For a fee, MITS would legally use the software. In return, MITS agreed to market, promote, and commercialize the software. Gates and Allen received royalties each time MITS licensed its software, even when the Altair or other hardware was not purchased along with it. The contract allowed them to collect a maximum of $180,000 in royalties. Once they received that amount, MITS would no longer have to pay royalties. The agreement also stated that Gates and Allen could terminate the contract if MITS did not hold up its end of the deal.

With a signed contract with MITS and brand new software ready to sell, Gates and Allen were finally living their dream as partners in a new business. And thus Microsoft was born. +

Flags fly high today at Microsoft headquarters in Redmond, Washington.

Allen and Gates shared a light moment at the annual
PC Forum in Phoenix, Arizona, in 1987.

SMALL SPACE, BIG PERSONALITIES

Microsoft was officially founded on April 4, 1975. The company's first office was located in the Albuquerque strip mall with MITS. Allen, still employed by MITS, split his time between MITS and Microsoft. In November, Gates arrived in Albuquerque to work with Allen. He took a leave of absence from Harvard, but he would never go back.

Gates spent some of his time traveling around the country visiting computer hobbyists who had formed clubs after purchasing Altair kits. He taught them about BASIC software at their club meetings, which were often in home garages or basements.

Though technically separate, Microsoft and MITS worked closely together. Gates and Roberts often clashed, arguing about everything from politics to current events to business practices. The two bullheaded personalities did not mesh. Roberts saw Gates as a spoiled kid, and Gates doubted Roberts's ability to make smart business choices. Allen, on the other hand, was well liked by Roberts and tended to keep peace between MITS and Microsoft.

THEY ARE STEALING MY PROGRAM

One of Microsoft's early challenges was software piracy. Gates was quite upset that instructions for writing Microsoft's BASIC software were being printed and distributed among computer hobbyists who owned Altairs. He was infuriated that any user could easily pirate the program he had worked so

MEDIA PIRACY

Copyright laws were passed in order to protect people's ideas, music, literary works, and software programs from being reproduced without the creator's permission. People profit from their artistic or intellectual creations, and when their works are copied and stolen, they lose money. Those who break copyright laws and use or reproduce a work without permission are commonly referred to as media pirates. Enforcing laws against piracy is complicated because sharing music and other creations is legal in countries such as Canada, Spain, Panama, the Netherlands, and Russia. Lawmakers and media producers have long debated who should be held responsible for copying music, movies, games, and the like. Many people wonder if the party at fault and guilty of illegal activity is the Web site that provides the download, the Web sites that have a link to that service, or the individuals who actually download the file or program onto a home computer. In March 2001, the popular file-sharing Internet service called Napster was ordered by a US court of appeals to stop sharing or trading copyrighted music on its Web site. Four months later, Napster shut down its network and paid music artists and producers $26 million in fines for its illegal music-sharing operation.

hard to develop. Gates was so passionate about this issue that he delivered a speech about it at the first and only World Altair Computer Convention in Albuquerque in March 1976. He spurred a lively debate among the 700 people who attended.

The reason hobbyists pirated was partly due to MITS's pricing model. Naked, or stripped, Altairs could be purchased very cheaply at just $150. They were much more expensive at $500 when installed with Microsoft software. The value of the machine was not so much in its body, but rather in its guts. Once hobbyists started stealing the software program, Microsoft's profits from the Altair diminished. At one point, Gates was so frustrated that he offered to sell Roberts the rights to BASIC for a measly $6,500. Lucky for him and the future of Microsoft, Roberts turned down his offer.

Though it irritated Gates that the BASIC interpreter was widely being stolen, it worked in Microsoft's favor in the long run. The BASIC interpreter became so widespread through pirating that it—and thus Microsoft—became the industry standard. "We set the standard" became Microsoft's company motto.[1] Later, the design of new hardware and programs worldwide would become based on compatibility with Microsoft's products.

NEW MEMBERS OF THE TEAM

Allen had exceptional intuition when it came to predicting market trends. He could see that Microsoft was going to grow, and early on, he hired programmers Steve Wood, Albert Chu, and Marc McDonald to join the company. Microsoft then began working on a software program on disks to replace the old punched paper tape that ran through a teleprinter. By November 1976, Allen had dropped his MITS gig to spend all his time with the rapidly growing Microsoft.

As the worldwide computer market grew, more computer manufacturers were making products that could benefit from Microsoft software. Microsoft, however, was restricted by the binding contract with MITS that prohibited Microsoft from selling its own software directly. Allen had to refuse offers from big brands such as Delta Data, Rand, and Magnavox because MITS had exclusive rights to the software. Usually, Roberts would not approve sales that would compete with any MITS product. Microsoft was also approaching the maximum $180,000 in total royalties it could earn under the contract. After it made that figure, Microsoft would not make any more money on its software installed on Altair computers. Gates began looking for a way out of the contract.

BREAKING WITH MITS

Microsoft claimed MITS had failed to promote the Microsoft software product. That, among other things, was reason enough for Microsoft to legally break its contract with MITS in 1977. Then Microsoft was free to sell its own software products to anyone. The Microsoft team began developing software for companies it had previously turned down, and money started flowing in rapidly.

One of the first deals Microsoft made was with the Tandy Corporation. Tandy's TRS-80 desktop computer, launched in 1980, used Microsoft BASIC to run its software programs. It was ready for use right out of the box. It did not need to be assembled from a kit. Sales soared at Radio Shack retail stores where the computers were sold. Microsoft also created a BASIC program for the Apple II computer.

XEROX

One of Microsoft's bigger contracts was a project for Xerox in 1979 that paid $150,000, which would be nearly $465,000 today. Though Gates was young, he managed to impress the Xerox executives with his technical expertise. At the time, Xerox was the industry leader in copying and printing.

Gates believed in the motto, "A computer on every desktop and Microsoft software on every computer."[2] His enthusiasm was catching, and the Microsoft team soon created an office atmosphere that accurately reflected the creative and youthful minds of the people who worked there. The dress code was mainly sneakers and jeans. Most of the male programmers wore beards. Hours were irregular, and the staff often worked late into the night. During breaks from long workdays, Allen played the guitar to unwind while Gates drove around town. He had a passion for vehicles and was known to sometimes break into closed construction sites at night and drive the equipment around.

GETTING BIGGER

Microsoft was growing at a phenomenal rate. On January 1, 1979, the company relocated from Albuquerque to Bellevue, Washington. On the way, Gates, ever the risk taker, received two speeding tickets. His energy continued at Microsoft's new office. Gates and Allen hired more programmers, including O'Rear, Bob Wallace, and Gordon Letwin.

Then Microsoft purchased its first minicomputer, a DEC 20, at a cost of $250,000. The Microsoft team then developed a BASIC program for Intel's new 8086 chip. The chip was faster and better than

BOB O'REAR

Bob O'Rear was a bit of a misfit in the Microsoft team. He was older than everyone else by at least ten years and was married. He did not work late nights, and sometimes Gates viewed this as a lack of commitment on O'Rear's part. However, Gates took advantage of O'Rear's age and maturity whenever the company needed to prove to a new client such as IBM that Microsoft was not just a bunch of goof-off kids.

Intel's first microprocessor is on display at the company's headquarters in Santa Clara, California.

any that had come before it, so Gates and Allen knew it would soon become the standard.

The Microsoft team presented BASIC for the 8086 at the National Computer Conference in New York City. People loved it, and the team celebrated in its hotel suite at the end of the night. They launched bottle rockets out the window over Central Park. A group of Japanese businessmen happened to join them. They could not get a room in the hotel that night since there was no vacancy. Gates and Allen invited them to crash on rollaway beds in their suite.

NISHI

Gates had a personal friendship and business relationship with Japanese businessman Kazuhiko Nishi that was profitable for both entrepreneurs for several years. It was Nishi who encouraged Gates to take on the job of creating the IBM operating system. But the two also conflicted. In 1986, they had a falling out over Nishi's lavish spending and impulsive conduct. Gates tried to resolve the spending issue by offering Nishi a job with Microsoft, but Nishi declined. When Gates and Nishi dissolved their business relationship, Nishi owed Microsoft $500,000, which Microsoft had never attempted to reclaim as of 2012.

The chance meeting with the Japanese businessmen helped Gates break into the Japanese market at the conference. He negotiated a deal with Kazuhiko Nishi, a fellow computer enthusiast, to distribute Microsoft products throughout Japan. Nishi brokered a deal with NEC, a Japanese technology company, to build a PC using Microsoft software. The PC 8001 was released in Japan, the United Kingdom, and the United States in September 1979.

Through Nishi's dealings, Microsoft managed to set the standard in the Japanese market as it had done in the United States. Microsoft had now made more than $1 million, but it was just getting started. A contract with IBM was just around the corner. +

Gates and NEC executive Yoshi Takayama appeared
together at a seminar in 1997.

In 1981, IBM marketed its first personal computer, Model 5150.

THE DEAL
OF A LIFETIME

Microsoft made an important international connection with Japan in 1979. But in 1980, Gates, Ballmer, and O'Rear were on their way to south Florida to make the deal of a lifetime with IBM. Microsoft had found an operating system that would run IBM's new PC. The deal with IBM would turn Microsoft into one of the world's most successful companies. In the months leading up to the public launch of the IBM PC, the gravity of how this deal would affect Microsoft finally hit Gates. Allen, on the other hand, had understood from the beginning that the ultimate game changer for the company would be an operating system distributed at high volumes.

Microsoft had been licensing 86-DOS from Seattle Computer Products for $25,000. When Microsoft adapted the operating system for the IBM PC, it came to be called MS-DOS—Microsoft's disc operating system. The people at Seattle Computer had no idea that a company as massive as IBM was Microsoft's client. Perhaps if Seattle Computer had known, they never would have accepted Microsoft's offer to buy 86-DOS for a mere $50,000. On May 1, 1981, Microsoft purchased full rights to 86-DOS and recruited and hired Tim Paterson, the programmer who had created it.

IBM unveiled its new PC on August 12, 1981, in New York City. Two weeks before, Allen had made one of the most famous deals of all time. He secured Microsoft's ownership of the operating system forever. Microsoft was not invited to IBM's rollout party for the PC, but it really did not matter because Gates, Allen, and the rest of the Microsoft team were celebrating on their own. MS-DOS was theirs, and they had an extraordinary deal with IBM to receive royalties for each sale of the IBM PC. Microsoft was also free to license it to anyone, including IBM's competitors. The following months led to massive growth for Microsoft.

By the end of 1981, sales of the PC with the MS-DOS version 1.0 operating system totaled 13,533. Each computer was priced between $1,500 and $6,000, and from those sales, Microsoft earned more than $16 million in just one year. By 1983, IBM had sold more than 500,000 PCs.

CREATING THE MANAGEMENT TEAM

Gates knew he needed more staff to handle such rapid growth. In 1980, he hired his old college friend Ballmer to help manage operations. While Ballmer was not a techie like the rest of the Microsoft team, he had excellent business intuition and management capabilities. Most important, Gates had enormous trust in him.

In 1981, Gates met Charles Simonyi through a mutual friend, Bob Metcalfe. Simonyi had an artistic passion for computer software and graphics, and the two hit it off right away. Simonyi had developed a computer for Xerox called the Alto. It was extremely functional and easy to use, and for a computer fanatic like Gates, it was a dream computer.

Gates hired Simonyi as director of advanced product development. Over the next two years, Simonyi created what would become Microsoft's most profitable product, an application for MS-DOS that helped computer users perform basic functions for work or school. His work was based in part on the VisiCalc spreadsheet application that had been independently created for the Apple II computer.

STEVE BALLMER

Steve Ballmer was born in Detroit, Michigan, in 1956. His father worked for Ford Motor Company. Ballmer received a scholarship to a reputable preparatory school, which was his eventual inroad to Harvard University. There, he met Gates. After graduating from Harvard, Ballmer worked for Proctor & Gamble for two years where he redesigned the Duncan Hines cake mix box. Ballmer once said, "I'm two things. I'm energetic and I'm bubbly. I wear it on my sleeve . . . energy, passion, willingness to throw yourself into things is essential."[1] His energy and intensity were part of the reason he connected so well with Gates. Though Ballmer is less technical and more of a charismatic spokesperson, the two men have shared a close friendship for many years. In 1980, Ballmer dropped out of graduate school at Stanford University to work for Gates as Microsoft's business manager. In the years that followed, Ballmer continued to be responsible for more operations at the company. Ballmer is now one of the wealthiest people in the world.

TIME'S MACHINE OF THE YEAR

In 1983, *Time* magazine named the computer the Machine of the Year. This was a departure from the regular annual Man of the Year format, which is now called Person of the Year. In the article, Roger Rosen-blatt wrote, "There's a New World coming again, looming on the desktop."[2]

Microsoft's new product included two programs—a word processing program, called Microsoft Word, and a mathematical spreadsheet program, called Excel.

As Microsoft was growing bigger and stronger, the company was shaken by very upsetting news. Allen was diagnosed with Hodgkin's disease, a form of cancer that would require intense radiation treatments and chemotherapy. In addition to his illness, Allen was showing signs of burnout due to the highly stressful atmosphere at Microsoft. Gates was saddened and disappointed when Allen decided to withdraw from full-time employment in 1982 so he could spend more time with his family. Allen beat the disease, but he did not stay with Microsoft. In 1983, he resigned to start his own software company, Asymetrix. Gates filled the gap by hiring Jon Shirley to serve as president of the company.

GEARING UP FOR GROWTH

In the mid-1980s, Steve Jobs, cofounder of Apple, became interested in what Microsoft was doing. Several years after the IBM PC was launched, Jobs dropped in on Gates and the Microsoft team. At the time, Apple was experiencing enormous success and had gone public on the stock market. Apple's stock soared, and Jobs became the youngest millionaire to ever make it to the Forbes 400 list of wealthiest Americans.

Although Jobs and his design-minded colleagues at Apple were not huge fans of the IBM PC, Jobs had a special project in mind for Microsoft. In 1984, Apple was getting ready to introduce the Macintosh computer, or the Mac, as it came to be called. The Macintosh featured a mouse, a new handheld device that users moved around on a flat surface next to the keyboard. The computer used a graphical user interface (GUI) so users could launch applications by pointing and clicking on images with the mouse, a technology pioneered on the very expensive Xerox Alto. It replaced the old method of typing word commands to interact with the computer. Jobs asked Microsoft to create three applications for the Macintosh—a spreadsheet, a business graphics

Steve Jobs, *left*, and Gates answered questions about Microsoft's spreadsheet at a press conference in New York City in 1985.

program, and a database. A connection had finally been made between Microsoft and Apple, the two most rapidly growing computer companies.

Meanwhile, as Microsoft continued growing and profiting from sales of the PC, IBM was facing fierce competition. IBM had used an open architecture hardware system to develop the PC. This meant that none of the individual parts that made up the computer were proprietary. Therefore, other computer companies such as Compaq quickly used IBM's ideas and developed similar PCs of their own. These companies took business away from IBM, but fortunately for Microsoft, they still had to license MS-DOS. While IBM's sales suffered, Microsoft's profits went up. Microsoft earned $10 million just from the companies who were selling clones of the original IBM PC.

THE SOFTCARD

Apple computers were run on an operating system that was different from Microsoft's. Basically, this meant the two types of computers did not speak the same computer language. In order for Apple II computers to run Microsoft software, Microsoft created the SoftCard. Plugging the SoftCard into an Apple II computer made it possible to use Microsoft software. In the early 1980s, approximately 100,000 SoftCards were sold, far surpassing Microsoft's expectations.

WE ARE MICROSOFT

Microsoft's extraordinary growth required even more new staff. Ballmer became responsible for recruiting. His strategy was to hire smart but green, or inexperienced, programmers who could be motivated to work intensely. His goal was to hire "little Bills."[3] Ballmer also recruited Vern Raeburn to head up consumer products. Raeburn quickly pulled together a team to market Microsoft's products more effectively. Sales and finance teams

MICROSOFT PRESS

In addition to its computer product lines, Microsoft launched Microsoft Press, a publishing division that created manuals for computing and various software usage. This helped the company establish an expert point of view and add value for its customers. Over the years, Microsoft would develop a program to better train its business executives and offer multiple ways for customers to receive service related to its products.

were established for the first time in the company's history. Microsoft also hired a full support staff for customer service and technical support.

Microsoft wanted to keep its employees a long time, so it established some incentives to make them stay. It offered stock options to some of the staff. When the company made more profits, the employees benefited. Gates already owned 53 percent of the company; Allen owned 31 percent. Ballmer, Raeburn, Simonyi, and Letwin each owned smaller percentages of Microsoft. The remainder was divided up among key management personnel, programmers, and investors. Stock options gave employees an incentive to work longer hours with no overtime pay in exchange for a payoff later when the value of Microsoft's stock went up.

NO TURNING BACK

Microsoft was now working on a new operating system for the PC. It was still based on MS-DOS, but it created a graphic environment on the computer screen. Computer users were growing increasingly interested in GUIs, especially after the 1984 launch of the Macintosh. The pictures and icons on the screen of a computer with a GUI operating system made navigation much easier. Microsoft's new operating system would be called Microsoft Windows. Word would be the core desktop application used with Windows. Gates hoped Windows would set the company ahead of competitors such as Apple. Gates announced Windows in 1983, but it would be two years before Microsoft would be ready to release it.

On November 20, 1985, Microsoft launched Windows with less than stellar reviews. Not only was the system embarrassingly late to the market, but it also tried to do more than the memory would allow and therefore ran slowly and inefficiently. Even worse, the development process had been so difficult and wrought with so much tension that Microsoft lost some of its best programmers and management staff along the way. For the first time, Gates faced public criticism.

In spite of Microsoft's troubles, the company was growing. That year, Microsoft celebrated its tenth anniversary, and the company had much to celebrate. There was no turning back. Gates plowed ahead in his quest to dominate the computer industry. He had a lot more to accomplish with Microsoft. +

Gates put Steve Ballmer, *left*, in charge of recruiting
some of Microsoft's most talented employees.

Gates presented Microsoft Windows in 1995.

A WINNING STRATEGY

Microsoft survived the problems with Microsoft Windows and the criticism that followed. But during the crisis, the company lost some of its influence. Internal turmoil erupted in the company. IBM refused to promote Windows, developing its own multitasking operating system called TopView. IBM also distributed VisiCorp's spreadsheet and word processing applications instead of Word and Excel.

Like a game of chess, each major computer company positioned its pieces to block the others from making a move. Each of them wanted to be in a position to win the game. In the case of Apple, Microsoft had to watch out for possible lawsuits. It avoided being sued by threatening to withhold development of Excel and Word for the Mac. Microsoft knew these programs could make or break Apple's sales. Microsoft was in a powerful position because it had already managed to secure the rights to use the GUI Apple had developed for the Mac. Gates then prevented Apple from releasing the MacBASIC programming language by not giving Apple a license to use Microsoft's BASIC.

One of Microsoft's triumphs was winning the ongoing competition for the best spreadsheet. Microsoft's Excel proved superior to the product developed by Lotus, its largest software competitor. When Windows 2.0 went to market in 1987, Microsoft sold it bundled together with Excel and Word. Selling the Microsoft operating system with

Microsoft software applications was a brilliant idea and the key to gaining market dominance.

GOING PUBLIC

Microsoft also had another idea that would guarantee its position at the top of the computer industry. In 1986, the company went public. Gates had never been interested in or trusted the stock market. But Microsoft had become too big to stay private. It had 500 shareholders, which meant it would have to follow government regulations that required it to publicly reveal information about company practices. Since it would have to open up its books anyway,

WINDOWS ROAST

When Microsoft finally launched the first retail version of Windows on November 20, 1985, the company held a roast instead of a regular party to celebrate. The purpose of the roast was to make light of the highly stressful past several months of development and acknowledge that the late release of Windows was a common joke in the industry. Gates told how Ballmer, "kind of a non-technical guy," came up with the idea to call it Microsoft Window.[1] Ballmer then hinted that even his job was on the line if the company had not eventually launched the product. Then Ballmer and Gates sang a song together—"The Impossible Dream"—as they stood arm in arm. The audience roared with laughter.

Gates appeared nervous, repeatedly pushing his eyeglasses up the bridge of his nose. He looked very young and slightly awkward in a tuxedo. Gates also demonstrated the operating system, showing how users could pull up different projects at the same time and resize objects and text.

Microsoft decided to go public, or offer its stock on the New York Stock Exchange.

Gates was not enthused about Microsoft's debut on Wall Street. But nearly everyone else with connections to Microsoft was abuzz with excitement. Gates received phone calls from his family doctor, his housekeeper, and others, begging for permission to invest in Microsoft before it went public. Not wanting to handle this kind of pressure, Gates left town on March 13, 1986, on a rare vacation to go sailing. That day, Microsoft went public, and its stock was sold on the stock market to the general public for the first time. Gates's 45 percent stake in the company was valued at $350 million. Within a year, Gates, Allen, and Ballmer were billionaires. Sixteen other Microsoft employees were multimillionaires.

VELVET SWEATSHOP

In 1989, Microsoft employees had special T-shirts made. On the front were the words "The Velvet Sweatshop."[2] The phrase poked fun at a *Seattle Times* article that suggested the company was overworking its employees to the point that it might be dangerous to their health and well-being. The article suggested employees were given a lot of perks such as food and entertainment as a way to disguise unfair demands.

In the midst of the competition and going public, Microsoft retained its lighthearted company atmosphere. But as Microsoft grew, some of the fun faded. The company focused on cleaning up its operations and becoming more efficient. Microsoft President Shirley reorganized the staff, fixed the accounting system, and reduced manufacturing costs. In an effort to expand its international presence, Shirley established subsidiaries in countries all over the world.

By the early 1990s, Microsoft had officially gone global. Separate business units were established, including Worldwide Product Development headed by Michael Maples, Worldwide Sales and Support led by Francis Gaudette, and Worldwide Operations directed by Ballmer.

With plenty of funds to spare, Microsoft could dabble in whatever aspect of the computer industry it chose. For now, it concentrated on adding products to Windows in order to gain more market share. When Microsoft shipped a Windows compact disc (CD) to a customer, other applications were included, such as Microsoft Bookshelf, a selection of reference books. When a customer inserted the CD into a PC, the applications became available on the computer's desktop.

WINDOWS FOREVER

The first few versions of Microsoft Windows operating system were fairly successful. They were what Microsoft would base its business on for the next several years. In 1990, Windows 3.0 was the first to achieve immediate and significant commercial success. Microsoft spent more than $10 million promoting Windows 3.0 on the most hyped media advertisement campaign ever seen by the computer industry. Then Windows 3.1 was launched with the new Windows flag logo, which became an icon of the company.

MICROSOFT UP, IBM DOWN

Microsoft also launched its strategy for what was referred to as the digital workplace. It developed a way for employees to connect or network their own PCs to a centralized computer. This allowed employees to login and

E-MAIL

Microsoft provided e-mail service for all of its employees. There were suspicions that executives were unofficially monitoring e-mail usage to determine whether or not employees were working over the weekends and late at night. But it was for a good purpose; those who were putting in extra hours were later rewarded with bonuses.

be connected to their businesses from various places in the office and eventually from remote locations. Microsoft purchased a license to use what was called an SQL server from a company called Sybase. The company had developed and marketed SQL along with a company called Ashton-Tate. The SQL server allowed these remote logins.

Eventually, Microsoft bought all rights to the SQL server and name. The server allowed Microsoft to compete head-to-head with IBM and other large companies that sold similar products. IBM was the company first responsible for Microsoft's onslaught into the operating system business. Now IBM was also Microsoft's largest competitor. But it was IBM that was suffering from the competition.

By 1993, IBM was losing billions of dollars and laying off staff in droves as most PCs were made by manufacturers of IBM clones. IBM was also hurt by the success of its competitors in the mainframe computer market. Microsoft and Intel had replaced IBM as the computer industry giants. Microsoft was looking forward to a bright future, but perhaps it was not looking as carefully as it should have. The decline of IBM and Apple should have come as a warning to Microsoft. +

Microsoft's smart business moves were increasing its prominence in the US economy and stock market.

Microsoft Excel and Microsoft Word were bundled with Windows
beginning in 1989 and sold on 90 percent of the world's computers.

ENEMIES
EVERYWHERE

Apple and IBM were not the only companies
that suffered because of Microsoft's incredible
success. Microsoft's license for use of the SQL
eventually made enemies of Sybase and Ashton-Tate.
The bundling of Excel and Windows hurt Novell

and Lotus. After rejecting an offer to partner up with Microsoft, Adobe complained that Microsoft was trying to stop it from creating software for Apple. Microsoft crushed a company called 3Com to the tune of $40 million over a royalty agreement. Still others, such as Micrografx and Go Corporation, claimed Microsoft had pretended to be interested in a partnership in order to steal trade secrets and develop competitive products. One small company called Z-Nix sued Microsoft for breaking an agreement to bundle the Z-Nix Super Mouse with Microsoft Windows. The two companies settled out of court.

Another major complaint was that Microsoft was guilty of marketing vaporware. This referred to an industry technique of announcing and promoting a product that was not yet developed. It allowed megacorporations such as Microsoft to gain a market foothold on technology that did not yet actually exist.

Eventually the rumblings of discontent among Microsoft's competitors found their way to the US government. Under the Sherman Act of 1890, the federal government is obligated to investigate any company suspected of anticompetitive practices. A Federal Trade Commission (FTC) investigation

A THREAT TO THE ECONOMY

During the investigation of Microsoft by the Federal Trade Commission, President Bill Clinton's administration encouraged Microsoft to resolve the case as quickly as possible. Gates reportedly told Vice President Al Gore that if Microsoft were ever split up, the company would simply move overseas. That would put the US economy at risk.

of Microsoft's business practices began in 1990. Microsoft seemed unfazed by the legal attention. Yet the worst-case scenario—that Microsoft might be broken up—would devastate the company.

A widely held belief in the computer industry was that Microsoft was attempting to monopolize everything from operating systems to software to the mouse. Microsoft appeared to be unstoppable. It was hard to fathom that Microsoft and its mastermind, Gates, could fail.

NETSCAPE IS COMING TO TOWN

Microsoft was doing very well with its focus on Windows, but a new phenomenon was brewing in the computer industry in Silicon Valley, California. The phenomenon was called the World Wide Web. A company called Netscape Communications owned the dominant technology to browse the World Wide Web.

Jim Clark and Marc Andreessen founded Netscape Communications in 1994. Clark had made his fortune in 3-D technology as the founder of Silicon Graphics, so he had the funds to begin a new venture. Andreessen had just graduated from the University of Illinois at Urbana-Champaign with a bachelor's degree in computer science. He also worked at the National Center for Supercomputing Applications (NCSA) at the university. It was at NCSA that Andreessen and his colleagues first discovered and developed the Mosaic browser technology for surfing the World Wide Web. When Andreessen and several colleagues left to form Netscape with Clark, the rest of the students at NCSA formed a similar company called Spyglass.

Gates had ignored warnings from his colleagues that the World Wide Web was going to be huge, but huge was an understatement. The Web took off almost instantly with 15 million users viewing a variety of Web sites on the Internet. Netscape developed Navigator, a Web browser that allowed users to retrieve information on the Web. Netscape rapidly soaked up 90 percent of the market within the first year. In 1995—the same year Microsoft launched Windows 95—the one-year-old Netscape went public. The company was valued at $3 billion.

IS MICROSOFT A MONOPOLY?

The FTC's initial investigation of Microsoft that began in 1990 ended in a deadlock, a 2–2 tie on whether to go after Microsoft as a monopoly. When the matter was turned over to the Department of Justice, Anne Bingaman, its newly appointed head, aggressively took on the case against Microsoft. Although the matter with Microsoft was not a lawsuit, federal judge Stanley Sporkin was assigned by lottery to review the agreement Bingaman wrote and wanted Microsoft to sign. This consent decree, as it was called, would place restrictions on Microsoft to prevent it from monopolizing the computer software market. Sporkin had a reputation for holding corporations accountable. Although he was known for being a bit loud spoken and unruly in the courtroom, he was considered a fair judge. On February 14, 1995, Sporkin rejected the 1994 consent decree reached with Microsoft and the Department of Justice the previous summer. Microsoft's enemies rejoiced. One IBM consultant even showed off a T-shirt at a conference with Sporkin's face on it. Above the judge's picture were the words, "Our Hero." However, on August 1, 1995, US District Judge Thomas Penfield Jackson reversed Sporkin's decision and approved the decree.

OFF THE HOOK?

Meanwhile, in 1994, the FTC had settled the Microsoft case out of court. Microsoft signed a consent decree in which it agreed not to bundle Windows with its software programs such as Word and Excel. The company could still add features to Windows or other operating systems.

Soon after Microsoft signed the decree, it tried to market Microsoft Money, a type of personal finance software. The program allowed users to manage their budgets and track

their expenses on the computer.
But Microsoft Money was never
profitable, since a company called
Intuit was marketing a very popular
finance management software
program called Quicken. Intuit's
product was simply superior to
Microsoft Money. Microsoft's
solution was to buy Intuit and own
the technology. But by the time
the company announced plans for
the merger, the US Department of
Justice was watching Microsoft's
every move. Antitrust lawyer Gary
Reback blocked Microsoft's buyout
of Intuit. The consent decree had not bothered Gates
very much. But this blocked acquisition of Intuit
was a message to Gates that his trouble with the
Department of Justice had just begun.

GATES ON INTUIT

When the US Department of
Justice blocked Microsoft's
buyout of Intuit, Microsoft was
forced to pay $46.25 million
for canceling the contract.
When Gates was asked how
this would affect his business, he said nonchalantly,
"The way this might affect our
business is that we'll probably
wait at least a week or two
before doing anything like this
again."[1]

UNITED STATES v. MICROSOFT

In August 1996, Netscape sent a letter to the US
government, claiming Microsoft was violating its
1994 consent decree by bundling Internet Explorer
with its Windows 95 operating system. In September,

the Department of Justice began investigating Netscape's claim. Microsoft had purchased a license from Spyglass to use the company's technology to create a Web browser. Now Microsoft was selling it packaged with Windows 95, referring to it as a feature rather than a product. With Internet Explorer included as a feature of Windows, there was no reason for people to use Netscape. Since Windows was on 90 percent of the world's computers, Microsoft essentially shut Netscape out of the market.

The Department of Justice filed a lawsuit against Microsoft, called *United States v. Microsoft*. It was the beginning of what would be referred to in the industry as the Browser Wars. The public began to have a different view of Microsoft and Gates. He was no longer the likeable though disheveled computer whiz; he was now viewed by many as a power-hungry,

GATES GETS MARRIED

During Microsoft's most difficult legal battle, longtime bachelor Gates decided to settle down with Melinda French, who worked for Microsoft. French oversaw 50 employees in the Microsoft Publisher division. Gates proposed to her on March 20, 1993. The news of their engagement traveled like wildfire over Microsoft's e-mail network. It inspired jokes from comedians and led the computer industry to speculate about whether Gates would finally relax and work a little less. The couple was married on January 1, 1994, in Hawaii. Gates's parents attended, although his mother died of cancer six months later.

money-grubbing monster. There was a growing disdain for Gates and Microsoft.

Microsoft hammered the final nail in Netscape's coffin when it intercepted the partnership between Navigator 2.0 and Sun Microsystems. Netscape wanted to use Java, Sun's programming language that could be run on any computer with any operating system—not just Windows. The partnership would threaten Microsoft's dominance in the market. So Microsoft used its industry pull and its cash to license Java itself.

Netscape sued Microsoft. Netscape tried to drum up support in the industry, a difficult task when basically every company that had been wronged by Microsoft was still dependent on the company for their businesses. A journalist for *Wired* magazine wrote, "The Microsoft trial was a war that neither side actually wanted to fight."[2] Eventually, Intel and Intuit testified against Microsoft. They were followed shortly thereafter by IBM and other companies. But it

INTERNET EXPLORER

The Mosaic browser Microsoft acquired from Spyglass became the basis for Internet Explorer. The browser allowed Microsoft to take the Internet browser market from Netscape. Nathan Myhrvold, head of Microsoft's Advanced Technology Group, was largely responsible for acquiring the browser. He pushed the company to focus on the Internet and go beyond Gates's interest in interactive TV and other products.

Attorney General Janet Reno met with reporters in May 1998 to announce the lawsuit against Microsoft.

would take the US government and 20 states to bring down Microsoft.

The trial against Microsoft began on May 18, 1998. The lawsuit, filed by the US Department of Justice and the attorneys general of 20 states, accused Microsoft of being a monopoly and blocking competition for its own profit. The lawsuit also claimed Microsoft had disobeyed the 1994 decree when it packaged Internet Explorer with its Windows operating system. Ironically, as the trial was going on, Microsoft was still toppling its competition. Netscape lost $88 million in revenue in 1998 because of Microsoft.

On November 5, 1999, US District Court Judge Thomas Penfield Jackson ruled that Microsoft did, indeed, have a monopoly in the PC operating systems market. On June 7, 2000, Judge Jackson issued his final ruling, ordering Microsoft to be split into two companies. One company would market the Windows operating system; the other would manage Internet Explorer and its other businesses.

The judge's decision in *United States v. Microsoft* sent shockwaves throughout the computer industry. The court found that Internet Explorer was not merely a feature of Windows and that Microsoft had violated the earlier court decree. Microsoft appealed the ruling immediately. The US government and 20 states in the lawsuit tried to convince the US Supreme Court to hear the case. But the nation's highest court refused and sent the case to a lower court, the US Court of Appeals for the District of Columbia.

On June 28, 2001, the appeals court reversed Judge Jackson's decision to break up Microsoft. The Department of Justice made a public statement on September 6 that it would no longer try to split up

Microsoft. On November 2, it reached an agreement with Microsoft and settled the case. As part of the settlement, Microsoft agreed to no longer form exclusive contracts or cut special deals with other companies. It also had to share its applications with other companies. Three people appointed by the court would have access to Microsoft's records and systems for five years. Many people viewed the settlement as little more than a slap on the wrist for Microsoft. Yet the case took its toll on the people behind the megacompany.

In the middle of the long, tiresome appeal, Gates resigned, ending his 25-year position as CEO of Microsoft. He took on the position of chief software architect and, on January 13, 2000, turned over leadership of the company to Ballmer. The government had failed to split up Microsoft, but Gates's resignation seemed to emphasize what the public and Microsoft's competitors were beginning to realize—Microsoft might be in danger. In 2001, a journalist wrote in his book about Microsoft, "We were already witnessing the end of Microsoft as we'd known it."[3] +

At a news conference on June 28, 2001, Gates said he was pleased with the court's decision to reverse the court-ordered breakup of Microsoft.

Microsoft introduced its new Windows 98 operating system in June 1998.

UNFAMILIAR TERRITORY

The years from 1995 to 2002 were not easy ones for the software giant Microsoft. The company had built its success on dominating the operating systems and software for the world's PCs. But desktop computers and software sold in a box were no longer as significant or important in the new Internet age of free information transfer. Other companies such as Google and Microsoft's longtime rival, Apple, were putting out products and services designed for the modern consumer of the information age.

Revenue in the computer industry was coming from advertising on Web sites where technology— and software—could often be obtained for free. While the rest of the world was embracing an era of rapid and open sharing of information and content, Microsoft was defensively trying to protect its products and information. It spent a good deal of time keeping its software from being circulated for free online. Critics suggested Microsoft's time would have been better spent looking for new and different opportunities.

EMPLOYEES LOSING STEAM

In the early 2000s, Microsoft began experiencing challenges familiar to many corporations once they hit a certain size and needed to maintain a certain percent of growth each year. Meetings and various department evaluations were zapping too much of programmers' time and pulling them away from creating new products. The company was too big, and employees were no longer creating new products quickly.

Microsoft employees were showing signs of discontent. Increasingly, the company was losing some of its best talent to competitors such as search-engine company Google and online retailer Amazon.com. Some of them left because Ballmer tried reducing operational costs by spending less on employee benefits, perks, and stock options. Employees had less hope of making millions on Microsoft stock as some of the early employees had done.

Some also claimed things at Microsoft had become somewhat stagnant. Gone were the days when developers willingly logged late-night and weekend hours, excited to put out new products. Now they were not confident the products they

LIKE IBM

In the 2000s, it seemed the once young, rebellious Microsoft had grown up to become much like the older, more established IBM. Both companies had struggled through antitrust cases. Both companies had consequently become fearful of being targeted again for violating the law. Each company changed its procedures to avoid more trouble. Microsoft in particular lost some of its spark and its tendency to take incredible risks. It lost some of those things that had once made it such a vibrant company. IBM transformed its focus to a new business—computer consulting services. It became the worldwide leader in this dynamic and rapidly growing business.

were creating would be the big, dramatic market blockbusters that MS-DOS and Windows were. A nine-to-five culture emerged with many employees eager to leave as soon as their eight hours were up.

PLAYING SOMETHING NEW

Microsoft began to adapt to the changing culture and make a move toward what was called webification. This effort was led in part by creative technologist J Allard. He had first alerted Gates in 1994 to the coming rise of the Internet. The subject line of his interoffice memo read, "Windows: The Next Killer Application on the Internet." In it he urged the company to "embrace, extend, then innovate" by repositioning Windows as a Web tool.[1] Allard helped the company first embrace the Internet through gaming. The Xbox video game console was his brainchild. It disrupted Microsoft's traditional development approach by not using the Windows operating system.

HOW XBOX GOT ITS NAME

The Xbox was originally called Direct X-Box. It was shortened to Xbox, a name the Microsoft marketing team members did not particularly like. They had a long list they thought were much better for the gaming console. The marketing people left the Xbox name on it during the testing period as one of the possible names for the new product. They expected consumers to reject the name, but in the end, Xbox was, without a doubt, the favorite name.

On November 14, 2001, Gates played with the new Xbox video game system at New York's Time Square the day before its launch.

On November 15, 2001, Microsoft launched Xbox in the United States. Microsoft hoped by creating a new gaming platform it would compete with Sony and others by "taking the best of the PC and putting it into a console."[2] It ended up achieving that goal via Xbox Live, which allowed users to play games online with broadband Internet service.

Games such as *Halo* and *Halo 2* helped Xbox Live grow to more than 20 million users by 2009. In addition to sales of the game console and the games, Microsoft brought in additional revenue with subscriptions to Xbox Live and the sale of headsets and other accessories. Games such as *Halo* became extremely popular, particularly with the online communities that formed around them. Players shared game tactics, posted to discussion boards, and more.

In September 2005, Microsoft launched the next generation Xbox 360. It ran on a different operating system than Xbox and allowed players to compete online. Users could also download games from the Internet, listen to music, and view television shows, movie trailers, and movies. Xbox 360 became a multi-billion dollar revenue driver for Microsoft.

HALO

Halo: Combat Evolved for Xbox was the first in a series of games that showed the effectiveness of the game's online platform. It developed such a following that when *Halo 2* was released, it brought in $125 million in sales on the first day, making it one of the most successful video games of all time. Microsoft later released *Halo 3* for Xbox 360.

MICROSOFT MAKES NEWS

Gaming was just one part of Microsoft's strategy for continued success. The company also entered the television market. In the late 1990s, Microsoft had developed a joint partnership with NBC to create the cable television channel MSNBC. Though NBC eventually bought Microsoft's share of MSNBC, Microsoft remained co-owner of the msnbc.com Web site.

Produced by Microsoft on its corporate campus, msnbc.com features online coverage of popular NBC News shows such as *Today* and *Dateline*. It also feeds stories from popular news publications such as *The Washington Post* and *Newsweek.* As a news source, msnbc.com has managed to attract significant online traffic and rival top competitors Yahoo! News and CNN.

IT'S NO iPOD

Although Allard's efforts with Xbox reaped many rewards, Allard was unable to help Microsoft become successful in the digital music market. In January 2007, Apple announced that computers were not the company's main focus anymore. Apple had launched the iPod in 2001 and iTunes in 2003, offering approximately 200,000 songs that could be downloaded from the Internet at $.99 each. That year, Apple also introduced its third-generation iPod that was extremely thin and light but held 7,500 songs.

Microsoft's attempt to compete with the iPod came in the form of Zune, launched in 2006. In addition to the handheld music playing device, Microsoft created the Zune Marketplace where Zune and Xbox 360 users could download songs, games, and other content. However, neither the product nor the service managed to put a dent in the massive success of the Apple iPod and the iTunes store.

When Microsoft released Zune in 2006, it was not completely ready. Microsoft had deliberately sped up the development and release of the product with a plan to make improvements later on. This had been a successful tactic in Microsoft's early days. But the

iTUNES

With its innovative music platform iTunes, Apple took advantage of a difficult market climate that threatened both hardware and software producers. Consumers were downloading music for free from Napster and other Web sites. While record companies were busy trying to sue for stolen music, Apple made it easier—and legal—for consumers to acquire and access music over the Internet. The iTunes platform allowed consumers to pay for music automatically and download songs and other content directly to their iPods and related devices.

first version of Zune froze, and the company tried unsuccessfully to fix it. Even with a second- and third-generation Zune, the product never gained mass-market appeal.

Microsoft had other setbacks in the early 2000s, too. One major flop was Windows Vista. The new operating system was supposed to be a breakthrough in revolutionary operating systems, but the slow process at Microsoft pushed back Vista's release so far that it was practically dead upon arrival to market. Consumers criticized the product while they became tired of waiting for it. Once Vista was out, some consumers complained about computer crashes and that the system used too much memory. Ballmer brushed off these incidents with the bold statement, "We won the desktop. We won the server. We will win the Web."[3] +

Advertisements promoted Microsoft Office and Windows Vista in 2007.

An unidentified demonstrator held up a sign calling for "Free software, Open source" following a speech by Gates at Beijing University in 2007.

OPEN-SOURCE THREAT

Microsoft wanted to embrace the Internet, but the so-called information highway was not always kind to Microsoft. The trend toward open-source software and technology made Microsoft's business more challenging. Open-source software, created by anyone with skills to create software, was free to the public. Users could change and improve the software and distribute it to others. Some open-source software was very similar to or the same as already existing software sold by companies such as Microsoft.

To meet the challenge, Microsoft built an open-source software strategy team and recruited Sam Ramji, who knew a lot about it. His job was to change public opinion that Microsoft was the enemy of open-source software. Ramji had his work cut out for him. He had the strange duty of helping Microsoft find a way to make money by giving away its software for free. He also rallied employees who loved open source and those who hated it. The debate over open-source software had polarized Microsoft employees. One important person Ramji had to win over was Microsoft's CEO, Ballmer, who had once compared open-source software to a "malignant cancer."[1]

OPEN-SOURCE SOFTWARE

Open-source software is software that anyone can develop, modify, and share for free. Though the term originally applied to source code—that is, the basis of the programming language used to create the software—it is now more widely used to refer to other technology that the consumer, rather than the copyright or license owner, has control over. The open-source software movement stresses the values of collaboration and anticommercialism.

Microsoft decided to take a risk online with free software and created a Microsoft Office application for the Web. It was a necessary and smart move. With a free Windows Live account, users could use an online version of Word and create and save documents to the Web site. One competitor of Windows Live was Google Docs, which similarly provided a way to save files online. Finally, it seemed Microsoft was responding to what open-source supporters had long been requesting.

ONGOING BATTLE WITH APPLE

Despite attempts to update its strategy and business practices, Microsoft continued to lose its footing in the stock market in 2010. It was also losing its ongoing battle with its biggest rival, Apple. Throughout the 1990s and early 2000s, Microsoft nearly crushed Apple, managing to dominate the entire computer industry. When Apple first asked Microsoft to build software applications for the Mac, Microsoft was a bigger and far richer company. But by 2006, Apple founder, Jobs, was turning down his nose at Gates. That year he insulted Microsoft by saying, "The only problem with Microsoft is that they have no taste. They have absolutely no taste."[2]

Whether or not there was any truth to the insult was not important. What mattered was that Apple was beginning to outdo Microsoft.

By May 2010, Apple finally had its revenge on its rival. For the first time, Apple surpassed Microsoft in stock market valuation. Apple was gobbling up the music market with iTunes and the electronic devices market with the new iPad. Apple's mobile market was extremely successful, with smartphone sales alone outselling PCs by 2011.

Microsoft had been trying to compete in the mobile market with the unsuccessful Kin smartphone. The company tried to win over the teen market with the flashy device. Unfortunately, two years and plenty of spending on development led to a meager 10,000 devices sold. Microsoft pulled the Kin from the shelves just six weeks after releasing it. Microsoft continues to try to make headway in the mobile market with the Windows Phone and tablet PCs with the Windows 8 operating system.

STEVE JOBS DIES

Like Gates and Microsoft, Steve Jobs was seen as the face behind Apple around the world. He was recognized for his bold, charismatic, and, at times, difficult management style. He also had a stubborn insistence on maintaining a certain standard of design and aesthetics, as well as a commitment to the platform. Jobs died of pancreatic cancer on October 5, 2011, at the age of 56. Although Jobs and Gates were longtime competitors, it is said they held a deep respect for one another's strength as leaders.

WINDOWS PHONE

Microsoft's mobile technology has been able to capture less than 2 percent of the market share, partly because Microsoft was so late getting into the smartphone market. In addition, Microsoft offers far fewer independently produced apps that make the Apple iPhone and iPad so popular.

In 2010, Microsoft laid off scores of employees. For the first time, sales and profits from Windows were down. It was reported that 2009 had been the company's "worst fiscal year since 1986."[3] These troublesome developments likely spurred two new major business ventures in 2010 and 2011, when Microsoft made remarkable moves in the Web and voice/video communications markets. The software giant was fighting for its position as the leader in the computer industry.

ARE WE ON TO SOMETHING?

Microsoft's track record in Web developments was not good. In 2008, Microsoft's attempt to purchase the Internet giant Yahoo! fell through. Microsoft tried a new tactic in June 2009 when it launched Bing, a new search engine intended to compete with Google. Bing was designed to sort the results of searches to give users the most important information first.

Microsoft introduced its Bing search engine Web site in 2009.

A relatively small percentage of Internet users ended up using or preferring Bing, but Microsoft continued promoting it, trying to make it grow. Google used similar features with its browsing technology and even copied some features from the Bing travel search. If Google was using a Bing feature, then perhaps Microsoft was on to something. Perhaps it was becoming more savvy with Web market trends and consumer needs. However, Microsoft had much ground to make up, as Google was used at that time for approximately two-thirds of all Internet searches in the United States.

On October 13, 2011, Microsoft purchased Skype, a service that allowed Internet users to communicate with people all over the world through real-time video and voice, for free. Skype users were logging hundreds of billions of minutes each year conducting friend-to-friend video communications, international video business conferences, and more. Microsoft spent a whopping $8.5 billion to purchase Skype. Its plan was to connect Skype to its Xbox 360 and to e-mail services such as Outlook.

As time goes on, the Microsoft corporate culture continues changing. Ballmer is making changes in the company to help Microsoft adapt.

MICROSOFT MILLIONAIRES

Microsoft was somewhat legendary for having made millionaires out of so many of its early employees. They saw themselves as "lottery winners."[4] After the company went public, it was not uncommon for employees to build lavish homes or show up at work in brand new sports cars. In-home theaters, indoor swimming pools, and tennis courts were popular. Extravagant vacations and donations to charity were also common. In the early 2000s, many who had become rich off of stock options were only in their forties. They still had plenty of time to pursue new ventures and opportunities. Some took quite creative paths. One programmer purchased a bowling league. Eventually he recruited talent from Nike to market the sport and the league, making it profitable for the first time. Another Microsoft millionaire, along with a small group of other former employees, formed a high-profile venture capital firm named Ignition Partners. And yet another employee launched a coffee business called Pure Vida.

In a 2009 interview with the *New York Times*, Ballmer discussed Microsoft's shift to a culture that will allow Microsoft employees to make more independent decisions and move forward on ideas and projects more quickly. Ballmer recognized that what had worked for Gates through the 1990s may no longer work in the twenty-first century.

GIVING BACK

Gates has been distancing himself more from the daily happenings at Microsoft. He increasingly devotes his time to his charitable organization, the Bill & Melinda Gates Foundation. Originally founded in 1994, the organization has focused on improving health around the world and bringing computers with Internet access to US libraries and low-income schools. The Gateses have raised more than $33 billion over the years for these causes.

The departure of Gates as CEO of Microsoft in 2000 symbolized a major transition for the software giant. It also marked the end of an era. Although Ballmer has been Microsoft's CEO for many years, Gates will most likely always be the face and the genius behind this extraordinary company. Microsoft's success did not come without a price.

It made enemies along the way. Smaller companies were often unable to compete with the giant. The company faced enormous legal battles, sometimes threatening its very existence.

Despite its struggles, Microsoft continues to be the dominant standard in both applications software and operating systems. The company still has tremendous financial resources and can afford to enter into partnerships and embark on a variety of creative ventures. And somehow, through everything, Microsoft's history has been marked by accomplishments that even the company's greatest enemies admire. +

Bill and Melinda Gates are known for their charitable work.

TIMELINE

1953	1955	1968
Paul Allen is born in Seattle, Washington, on January 21.	William Henry Gates III is born in Seattle on October 28.	Gates and Allen meet at Lakeside School.

1981	1983	1983
The IBM PC with MS-DOS is launched on August 12.	Allen resigns from Microsoft.	Microsoft Word is launched.

1975

In March, Gates and Allen create a programming language for the first microcomputer, the Altair 8800.

1975

Gates and Allen found Microsoft on April 4.

1981

In June, Microsoft purchases the rights to QDOS from Seattle Computer and incorporates in the state of Washington.

1984

Apple creates the Macintosh computer and Microsoft provides the software.

1985

Windows is launched on November 20.

1986

Microsoft goes public on March 13.

TIMELINE

1990	1990	1994
The Federal Trade Commission starts an investigation of Microsoft's antitrust practices.	Windows 3.0 launches in May to rave reviews.	Gates founds the William H. Gates Foundation; he renames it the Bill & Melinda Gates Foundation in 2000.

2000	2001	2001
A federal judge orders Microsoft to split into two companies on June 7.	The Department of Justice and Microsoft settle the antitrust case on November 2; Microsoft remains a single entity.	Microsoft enters the gaming market with Xbox on November 15.

1995

Windows 95 launches with the Internet Explorer browser in August.

1996

The US Department of Justice investigates Netscape's claim that Microsoft is bundling Internet Explorer with Windows 95.

2000

Gates resigns as CEO on January 13, and Steve Ballmer takes his place.

2005

Microsoft launches Xbox 360 in September.

2009

Microsoft launches Bing in June.

2011

Microsoft purchases Skype on October 13.

ESSENTIAL FACTS

CREATORS
Bill Gates (October 28, 1955–)

Paul Allen (January 21, 1953–)

DATE LAUNCHED
April 4, 1975

CHALLENGES
United States v. Microsoft was one of the largest and most publicized antitrust cases in the history of the computer industry. Though the initial verdict on the case was to split Microsoft into two entities, the final settlement allowed the company to remain a single entity but abide by new regulations with regard to contracts and product marketing.

Throughout the 2000s Microsoft has struggled with open-source software downloaded for free from the Internet, which cuts into its profits. In the late 2000s, the company developed a strategy to make its software products available and able to be stored online.

SUCCESSES

Microsoft Windows 3.0, launched in May 1990, achieved incredible market success. The operating system became the standard, with 90 percent of the world's computers using MS-DOS or Windows. Microsoft outdid its competition and became the leader in software applications such as Word and Excel as part of the Microsoft Office Suite. Its success was due in part because it packaged and sold its software with its operating system. Microsoft launched Internet Explorer, which it sold with Windows 95. The company entered the gaming industry and introduced the enormously successful Xbox and Xbox 360. Microsoft continues to embark on successful initiatives such as voice and communications technologies with its purchase of Skype, interactive media through its association with NBC, and intuitive search engine technology with its launch of Bing.

IMPACT ON SOCIETY

Microsoft has set the dominant standard in software and operating systems for personal computers all over the world. The Bill & Melinda Gates Foundation has provided more than $33 billion to social justice and charitable causes around the globe.

QUOTE

"We set the standard."

—*Microsoft slogan*

GLOSSARY

antitrust

Opposing monopolies, especially with a view to maintaining and promoting competition.

application

Computer software designed to help the user perform tasks.

binary code

Code that uses unique combinations of the digits 0 and 1 to represent text and other characters.

byte

Eight bits of computer data that together represent a character, number, or color.

chip

A small piece of electronic equipment used to carry out a number of electronic functions in an integrated circuit.

memory

Where data and program information is stored on a computer for later retrieval and use.

microcomputer

A small computer meant for personal use; commonly called the personal computer.

minicomputer

A midrange computer that lies between a mainframe computer and a microcomputer.

monopolize

To control by preventing others from participating.

open architecture

A type of computer or software that allows adding, upgrading, and swapping components.

pirate

To use someone else's work without permission.

proprietary

Owned and controlled exclusively by an individual or corporation.

software

The programs used to direct the operations of a computer.

stock option

Opportunity a company gives its employees to purchase stock in the company.

subsidiary

A company under the control of another.

valuation

The estimated worth of a thing.

vaporware

Software that has been advertised but not yet produced.

webification

Adaptation of a product to a digital or Web-based format.

ADDITIONAL RESOURCES

SELECTED BIBLIOGRAPHY

Bryant, Adam. "Meetings, Version 2.0, at Microsoft." *New York Times*. New York Times, 16 May 2009. Web. 27 Jan. 2012.

Greene, Jay. "The Soul of a New Microsoft." *BusinessWeek*. Bloomberg, 4 Dec. 2006. Web. 27 Jan. 2012.

Heilemann, John. "The Truth, the Whole Truth, and Nothing But the Truth." *Wired*. Condé Nast, Nov. 2000. 8.11 (2000). Web. 27 Jan. 2012.

Wallace, James. *Hard Drive: Bill Gates and the Making of the Microsoft Empire*. New York: Harper Paperbacks, 1993. Print.

Wallace, James. *Overdrive: Bill Gates and the Race to Control Cyberspace*. New York: Wiley, 1998. Print.

FURTHER READINGS

Aaseng, Nathan. *Business Builders in Computers*. Minneapolis, MN: Oliver Press, 2000. Print.

Hunnewell, Lee. *Internet Piracy*. Minneapolis, MN: Abdo, 2007. Print.

Richardson, Adele. *The Story of Microsoft*. Mankato, MN: Smart Apple Media, 2004. Print.

Strother, Ruth. *Bill Gates*. Minneapolis, MN: Abdo, 2007. Print.

WEB LINKS

To learn more about Microsoft, visit ABDO Publishing Company online at **www.abdopublishing.com**. Web sites about Microsoft are featured on our Book Links page. These links are routinely monitored and updated to provide the most current information available.

PLACES TO VISIT

Computer History Museum
1401 N. Shoreline Boulevard
Mountain View, CA 94043
650-810-1010
http://www.computerhistory.org/
The Computer History Museum is the world's premier museum documenting and exploring the history of computing and its impact on society.

Microsoft Visitor Center
15010 NE Thirty-Sixth Street
Microsoft Campus, Building 92
Redmond, WA 98052
425-703-6214
http://www.microsoft.com/about/companyinformation/
visitorcenter/en/us/default.aspx
The Microsoft Visitor Center features the sights and sounds of the Microsoft legacy and displays hands-on exhibits of some of the company's latest technologies.

SOURCE NOTES

CHAPTER 1. SOFTWARE START-UP TO SUPERSTAR
None.

CHAPTER 2. BORN TO SUCCEED
1. James Wallace. *Hard Drive: Bill Gates and the Making of the Microsoft Empire*. New York: Harper, 1993. Print. 12.

2. Ibid. 25.

3. Paul Allen. *Idea Man: A Memoir by the Cofounder of Microsoft*. New York: Portfolio, 2011. Print.

CHAPTER 3. FLEDGLING COMPANY
1. James Wallace. *Hard Drive: Bill Gates and the Making of the Microsoft Empire*. New York: Harper, 1993. Print. 67.

CHAPTER 4. SMALL SPACE, BIG PERSONALITIES
1. James Wallace. *Hard Drive: Bill Gates and the Making of the Microsoft Empire*. New York: Harper, 1993. Print. 120.

2. Ibid. 153.

CHAPTER 5. THE DEAL OF A LIFETIME
1. Adam Bryant. "Meetings, Version 2.0, at Microsoft." *New York Times*. New York Times, 16 May 2009. Web. 20 Dec. 2011.

2. Roger Rosenblatt. "A New World Dawns." *Time*. Time, 3 Jan. 1983. Web. 5 Mar. 2012.

3. Stephen Manes. *Gates: How Microsoft's Mogul Reinvented the Industry—and Made Himself the Richest Man in America*. New York: Touchstone, 1994. Print. 177.

CHAPTER 6. A WINNING STRATEGY
1. "History of Microsoft." *YouTube*. YouTube, Web. 5 Mar. 2012.

2. Paul Andrews. "Inside Microsoft—A 'Velvet Sweatshop' or a High-Tech Heaven?" *Seattle Times*. Seattle Times, 23 Apr. 1989. Web. 6 Mar. 2012.

CHAPTER 7. ENEMIES EVERYWHERE

1. James Wallace. *Overdrive: Bill Gates and the Race to Control Cyberspace*. New York: Wiley, 1998. Print. 263.

2. John Heilemann. "The Truth, the Whole Truth, and Nothing but the Truth." *Wired*. Condé Nast, Nov. 2000. Web. 15 Dec. 2011.

3. John Heilemann. *Pride before the Fall: The Trials of Bill Gates and the End of the Microsoft Era*. New York: Collins Business, 2001. Print.

CHAPTER 8. UNFAMILIAR TERRITORY

1. Jay Greene. "The Soul of a New Microsoft." *Businessweek*. Bloomberg, 4 Dec. 2006. Web. 3 Jan. 2012.

2. "Xbox Brings 'Future-Generation' Games to Life." *Microsoft News Center*. Microsoft, 10 May 2000. Web. 1 Jan. 2012.

3. Jay Greene. "Troubling Exits at Microsoft." *Businessweek*. Bloomberg, 26 Sept. 2005. Web. 28 Dec. 2011.

CHAPTER 9. OPEN-SOURCE THREAT

1. Cade Metz. "How Microsoft Learned to Stop Worrying and (Almost) Love Open Source." *Wired*. Condé Nast, 4 Nov. 2011. Web. 28 Dec. 2011.

2. Jay Greene. "The Soul of a New Microsoft." *Businessweek*. Bloomberg, 4 Dec. 2006. Web. 3 Jan. 2012.

3. "Microsoft Corporation." *New York Times*. New York Times, 29 Nov. 2011. Web. 3 Jan. 2012.

4. Jule Bick. "Microsoft Millionaires Come of Age." *New York Times*. New York Times, 29 May 2005. Web. 28 Dec. 2011.

INDEX

INDEX CONTINUED

ABOUT THE AUTHOR

Ashley Harris lives in Chicago, Illinois, where she works as director of corporate relations at a leading design graduate school. She has authored several books for adolescents, including *Tupac Shakur: Multi-Platinum Rapper* and *Arms Trade*, and books in the Essential Health: Strong, Beautiful Girls series. Her work has appeared in *Time Out Chicago* and *Venuszine*. She holds a master's degree from the University of Chicago.

PHOTO CREDITS

Justin Sullivan/iStockphoto, cover; Ron Wurzer/Getty Images, 6, 24, 96, 97 (top); IBM/AP Images, 10; Ted S. Warren/AP Images, 13, 85; AP Images, 14, 56, 99 (top); Bettmann/Corbis/AP Images, 19; Evan Agostini/AP Images, 23; Heinz Nixdorf Museumsforum/AP Images, 28; Joe Brokert/AP Images, 33; Ann E. Yow-Dyson/Getty Images, 34, 55; Tony Avelar/Bloomberg/Getty Images, 41; Shizuo Kambayashi/AP Images, 43; INTERFOTO/Alamy, 44; Andy Freeberg/Getty Images, 50; Lynsey Addario/AP Images, 63, 97 (bottom); Scott Eklund/Liaison/Getty Images, 64; Susan Walsh/AP Images, 72; Cheryl Hatch/AP Images, 75; Jeff Christensen/Getty Images, 76; Jeff Christensen/AP Images, 80, 98; Elizabeth Dalziel/AP Images, 86; Newscast Limited/AP Images, 91, 99 (bottom); Eric Piermont/AFP/Getty Images, 95